Flat Belly

Healthier, Leaner, Happier

By Michael Chapman

http://PersonalityDevelopmentMastery.com

PERSONALITY DEVELOPMENT MASTERY

© 2016 Michael Chapman

All rights reserved. No part of this publication may be reproduced, stored in a retrieval system, or transmitted in any form or by any means, electronic, mechanical, recording or otherwise, without the prior written permission of the author.

Personality Development Mastery - 2016

DISCLAIMER

This book details the author's personal experiences with and opinions about right-brained learning. The author is not licensed as an educational consultant, teacher, psychologist, or psychiatrist.

The author and publisher are providing this book and its contents on an "as is" basis and make no representations or warranties of any kind with respect to this book or its contents. The author and publisher disclaim all such representations and warranties, including for example warranties of merchantability and educational or medical advice for a particular purpose. In addition, the author and publisher do not represent or warrant that the information accessible via this book is accurate, complete or current.

The statements made about products and services have not been evaluated by the U.S. government. Please consult with your own legal or accounting professional regarding the suggestions and recommendations made in this book.

Except as specifically stated in this book, neither the author or publisher, nor any authors, contributors, or other representatives will be liable for damages arising out of or in connection with the use of this book. This is a comprehensive limitation of liability that applies to all damages of any kind, including (without limitation) compensatory; direct, indirect or consequential damages; loss of data, income or profit; loss of or damage to property and claims of third parties.

You understand that this book is not intended as a substitute for consultation with a licensed medical, educational, legal or accounting professional. Before you begin any change in your lifestyle in any way, you will consult a licensed professional to ensure that you are doing what's best for your situation.

This book provides content related to educational, medical, and psychological topics. As such, use of this book implies your acceptance of this disclaimer.

Table of Contents

Introduction

Thanks for taking the time to download The Flat Belly Diet!

My name is Michael Chapman, and throughout this eBook you are going to get access to a wonderful range and selection of solutions that can help you get rid of that fat belly, and turn it into a flat one!

All you need to do is start reading from this section on. We've broken down a gluttony of various solutions that all can help to contribute to a better quality of life for you in the future.

By using the various suggestions that we have for you, then you can see progressive improvement long-term.

For more information and advice about how to make the most of your situation, we recommend that you read through this book. Every section has been prepared to help you get a great tip that is sure to help you finally deal with your issues regarding a belly gone big!

You'll be learning vital skills such as:

- The importance of the right kind of body management. From getting the right amount of sleep to simply laughing a lot more, the solutions that you need exist. We'll help you see how slowing down the overall pace of life can help you to be far better at adapting to improving your body.

- The right way to eat, and the right styles. Whether it's learning to eat as you wake or to try and give you a more peaceful sleep, many solutions exist which we have listed for your enjoyment.

- What you should be eating, from boosting your protein intake right through to using a zero sugar diet.

- Smart tips like using lemon water and low sodium salt to give ourselves treats that are good for us

- The importance of smart features like chewing heavily to simulate satisfaction or cutting out things like soda that will make our lives much harder. Want an easy way to make your life easier? Then follow the various tips included for an improved quality of life.

- Making sure that you have the right kind of fitness programs to work on, and making sure that your body has the correct intake. For more information and advice, be sure to check out the various fitness programs listed in here.

By using the information that we provide you will be much closer to building the kind of body, and proportion of belly, that you had always wanted. Our tutorials will help you:

- Feel far more comfortable with who you are and how you look. This will greatly improve the speed of which you'll feel confident.

- Begin to see that an end is in sight – there is no magic trick to getting into shape. It takes hard work and the vision to see that.

- Move towards giving your body a much greater level of strength and control than ever before. With our program you will be able to keep your body looking sublime!

- Feel healthier in the mind as well as the gut.

Does this sound like the kind of benefits you want to have? Then let's get involved – change is just around the corner!

Sleep 7+ Hours

The first and most important ally that you can bring to the table here is sleep. I found that one of my major problems for having such a big belly was my propensity to stay up at night until silly o'clock. To avoid this, I started working on learning how to sleep at more regular and respectable timelines.

Before long I found myself handling sleep much better than I had in the past. It just took a simple re-adjustment of the time I would go to bed at. I used to go to bed at 2AM, now I go to bed at 12:30-1AM. This makes a HUGE difference the next day as I now get my 7 hours minimum.

In the mornings I wake up and feel energized, enlightened and far happier than I had been the day before. But if you can't adjust your sleeping pattern, try and eat some more meats with Tryptophan in it.

This is an amino acid found in lamb and turkey, and is like a sleep tablet. Just ¼ gram of it which you will find in skinless chicken drumsticks or 3oz of turkey meat is enough to make us sleep better.

Now, when you go to bed, you are likely to get a deeper sleep that is less likely to be affected. When we sleep properly we have more energy the next day, reducing the amount of food that we need to consume to stay energized. With a 6% drop in calorie intake when we sleep properly, we can literally change our lives here.

All it takes is a desire to change how you eat and sleep. 120 calories per day can be cut off from an average 2,000-calorie lifestyle. Over a month, that's a pound! It's small gains, but every little will help.

Laugh

Laughter is more powerful than any diet – as soon as I discovered how laughter could help make that belly vanish, I worked on it. Apparently, an hours' worth of laughter is the same to us as doing a small aerobic workout!

Laughter makes the heart beat faster and means that our body starts pumping blood out at a level it has never done in the past. Naturally, this will improve our uptake on the stomach muscles. Since we are convulsing with laughter, and our chest will rise and fall as we laugh, we are actively working on tightening that part of our body up

I found the best way to work on this was to get on YouTube. You can find hours' worth of hilarious comedians and skits that will leave you in fits of laughter. We all have our own tastes in comedy so I won't try and make suggestions but, believe me, this is far more powerful than it may sound to you at this moment in time.

Start to laugh more regularly and your belly flab won't stand a chance. An hour of solid enjoyment and comedy a night makes us happier, but also makes us thinner!

Practice Mindfulness

One tool that I found really effective was to practice mindfulness. In my early journeys to understanding and fully appreciating the power of losing my flat belly, I had to learn about my whole mentality. It turns out that, in my earliest days, I spent a lot of time of just eating what seemed quickest for me.

By being more mindful, I could make sure that I avoided lapsing and making silly errors as I tried to adjust my diet. The best way to adjust to mindfulness and to practice it, I found, was to simply understand the current state of mind you have.

Basically, by always being present in the moment and being aware of your thoughts about a situation, you can control that situation. When you feel hungry it might be reflex to head to Subway or to make a fry-up. However, if you are mindful of this then you can pay attention, avoid eating that kind of crap, and instead eating a "real" meal.

I found that by being mindful I made my life much easier. Mindfulness can be practiced by simply honing your mind to look at your thoughts in a more retrospective manner. To be more mindful, pay attention to food colouring, textures, styles, tastes, smells and everything else associated with that fine.

By doing that you become more alert to each kind of food – and how it makes you feel. Still unsure?

Then try out these mindfulness audio files from Reboot with Joe for help.

Slow Down Your Pace To Reduce Stress!

One major lifestyle change that I made to my life was to reduce stress by slowing down. You might think this sounds counterproductive – how do I slow down but still get the same amount of things completed every day?

The reason I turned to being slower in pace is that I found that, when I panicked, I turned to food. I would become stressed and eat something. Or I would get angry, rush the project/job/task, make a mess of it, have to re-do it, waste my time and then would eat junk food to cheer myself up.

It's a vicious cycle!

So, the easiest way to correct this mental oversight for me was to slow down. Take tasks more methodically and stop trying to run through everything at 100mph. I started to finish tasks at the right time of the day and in the right quality.

My personal and professional life improved. I was way less stressed than I was in the previous years and just felt much happier with who I was, and where I wanted to be in life. It was a simple alteration but one that made a huge difference to my life.

I felt less stressed so my body went through less trouble. My quality of life improved, my binge eating desires vanished, and my belly started to do the same!

Slowing down the pace of my day was probably the smartest thing that I have ever done. It made me a happier person, more professional, and more likely to get jobs done. Now, I look better, get more finished and work at a pace that avoids stress eating.

Eat Peacefully

If you have kids, or you happen to live in a busy area, then you might find this one hard to do. I found that the easiest way to eat is when we have no distractions. No noise outside, no kids talking, no other problems going on around us. Simply by eating in this manner I could make sure that I ate properly. Eating peacefully is very important, I found, because it helps to settle the body.

However, to eat peacefully, you need to be able to be at peace with your own mind. Many people struggle with this as they find themselves always beating themselves up. Whenever I had a "slip" and would eat something bad for me, I would punish myself for hours.

This made me feel quite uncomfortable in my own mind and ruined the enjoyment of eating for me. To eat peacefully, you have to be at peace with the idea of eating. People worry themselves sick of overeating, eating without purpose...this, though, just creates a poor quality of life.

I found that by simply eating in a quiet environment, I could then contemplate in my mind why it was such a big issue to eat. Even when eating healthy meals I would find myself going over it in my mind, making a problem where there should not have been one.

To eat peacefully, you need peace both in and around the world near you and in your mind. Shut down the inner monologue, and find silence. Only then can you truly enjoy eating your food – remember, we are here to learn how to eat the right foods for a flat belly.

Eat When Waking

Given my lifestyle, I used to be terrible for not eating in the morning. In fact, in the past, my first meal of the day would be lunch – on bad days, it was dinner!

The most effective time to eat, I found, was within an hour of waking up. This is apparently the most effective ways to do so is because I – and others – make up for waiting so long to eat later. The longer you are up the less hungry you may become and if you have things like coffee or cigarettes, this will only become worse.

Therefore, having something to eat within an hour or waking is going to make your life so much easier than it has been in the past. Within that one hour time frame you should be trying to eat as it also helps us wake up and attack the day.

You are more alert and easier to deal with when you eat within that first hour. Now you have satisfied a major urge and can get on with your day, making it easier. I used to be terrible for this and would make it worse by eating more and more as the day went on.

Within that first hour the window for eating is vital. If you don't then you will find that – like me – your mood is nowhere near as balanced as it could, or should, be. Make yourself more balanced mentally by making the change and you'll find that the mornings are no longer as irritating!

Efficient Protein Times

There are, apparently, good and bad times to take in protein. The best time for most people is in the morning (see the next idea). However, the best times to undertake this usually means enjoying efficient protein bonuses that would not have existed outside of this. Try going between 3-4PM if your lifestyle allows it.

This hour of the day is the most important time to get a protein snack down you because this is the hour that the body metabolises and balances your blood sugar. Food coming in every 3-4 hours is the best way to balance our blood sugar levels, but protein-based meals between these hours is going to be a huge benefit for you.

Now you can boost your metabolism for the rest of the day and burn off more at a quicker rate just by having this little ally alongside you. As far as making your life easier and being more efficient, you will find that these times are going to play a major role in making that so.

Balanced blood sugars means that your insulin levels will be lower, which is important. With a higher insulin level your body feels happy and OK – this means it starts to store fat. In the belly!

As soon as I found this out I made the change – immediately. I started eating at the right times and made sure that with a more balanced insulin level throughout the day my body was bound to enjoy itself far more, and also store far less.

Having a High Protein Breakfast

One of the major changes that I began to make to my lifestyle was having a more high-protein existence. One reason why I began to do this was so that I could enjoy a more comprehensive and comfortable lifestyle. It also meant that by starting the day in this way, I was giving my body the energy it needs to start the day in the right manner.

I used to wake up and run on Corn Flakes and Orange Juice. The problem was that this just gave me really high sugar content and by 11AM I would have my head on the desk. My mind was blank and running on empty – I'd burned through all of that cheap energy in a matter of hours.

Then, I turned to a high-protein breakfast that consisted of things like real cereals with milk. No more Corn Flakes or Frosties, instead replaced by High Fiber cereals instead. I would then add some sunflower seeds into the dish and just scoff it all down – this added more protein to the meal.

Another option was egg and cheese on a whole roll or wrap. An egg burrito breakfast roll is bound to give me plenty of positivity with around 25g of protein on offer with most egg-based dishes. Two scrambled eggs, some black beans and a few sautéed onions was all that I needed to make breakfast give me the energy that I was lacking.

Now, days were more productive and breakfasts stopped expanding my waistline at all!

Zero Sugar Diet

The best solution I can probably offer to you, though, is the 'zero sugar' diet. You can read more about a form of this plan from LIVESTRONG here. Not only is going on a no sugar diet very good for your body to detox, for those who want to reduce belly size it can be an amazing life change.

Cut it out of your tea and hot drinks. Ban sugary snacks and meals. Get soda out of the house. This is a genuine fast-track to making your life more balanced than it was in the past. You also reduce the chance of that belly from expanding – sugar is one of the key culprits in making us expand to an uncomfortable size.

Cutting out nonsense like soda, sweet teas, cakes, cookies, candy, chocolate and the like is an absolute must if you want to make this form of dieting a success.

I found that by cutting out sugar from my diet I feel healthier and have removed a major source of weight gain. With this done I can feel a whole lot more comfortable about managing my weight and beginning to make sure I feel comfortable, happy and healthy.

Drinking Lemon Water

I found that when I first started to go on this kind of flat belly killing regime, that my body was HATING it. It just seemed to make me feel awful!

However, one of the most powerful solutions I could recommend to you is drinking room temperature lemon-infused water. For one, a lemon contains just shy of double – 187% - of our daily requirement of Vitamin C. since the body gets rid of the rest of the stuff we don't need, it's safe to take this amount in.

This gives our body's incredible ways to strengthen our immune systems as well as make sure you feel more energised. By using room temperature water with lemon, you give your body more energy. It's refreshing, sure, but it's actually good for getting those energy levels up. As you adjust to a new way of eating and living you will feel lethargic, and this can help you bridge that gap moving forward.

Also, lemon water allows you to make your body more alkalized. A balance in the body is vital as most illnesses apparently form in an acidic environment. Whilst lemon juice is acidic, the fruit is one of the most alkaline foods we can ever take.

A good cup of room temperature water with the juice from half a lemon is enough to make your mornings brighter and more exciting. Using this and you'll feel more alert, meaning you avoid from using sugary treats and goods to "perk yourself up" and thus make your gut more likely to be harmful.

I would recommend this as a #1 priority. It's super powerful and makes sure that your body is going to be very useful for removing the acidity that causes so many problems. By having a better pH balance you are looking after your body, whilst also reducing dependence of gut-building snacks for energy.

Low Sodium Salt

One part of my health planning that I found out was that we need salt. I thought that by just cutting salt out of my life I would be healthier and happier for it. However, our bodies do need some salt – it's just that most of us (me included) have salt with the food as the topping.

Too much salt is terrible for us; it weakens our bodies, hardens our arteries and just makes our bodies feel much worth.

However, you can easily fix this by using low sodium salt instead. Whilst I still would never recommend using the same volumes as you may do already, low sodium salt allows you to still enjoy it. A tiny sprinkling of low-sodium salt over a meal can make it come to life and taste better than ever before.

Some meals just don't come to life until you put some salt on them. Some things just need that bit of extra character and taste. Salt works as a wonderful way to make the taste come out of a product as you would have hoped for.

This was probably my hardest part of changing – getting used to food without salt. I found most of my meals now tasted bland and average. The addition of using low sodium salt, though, makes such an incredible difference.

Now my meals would still taste wonderful whilst making sure that you can enjoy and appreciate the power of reducing belly fat without high sodium salt.

Chewing a Lot

As someone who used to chew like an owl (i.e. I didn't) I found it very useful to start chewing a lot. Chewing does two major things for us;

- Makes it easier for our bodies to digest the food. When we are chewing we find that we can reduce the overall drama and tension of the food in our digestive system by chewing it.

- Since you are basically turning the food into a paste by chewing it, it soon becomes a whole lot easier to chew down on.

- Also, chewing does something wonderful for us – it makes us feel full. By chewing and chewing and chewing, you make your food much easier to go down.

- Crucially, you also make a signal to the brain that you were fully satisfied about the food that you have just enjoyed. It quite literally removes the need to keep eating as it makes you feel happy with what you ate.

Since I used to just swallow my food with minimal work and chewing, I would rarely feel full. I could even eat leftovers from other plates. It was only later on in the night when my stomach felt like it was going to pop, that I would regret doing so.

I completely changed around the quality of life that I live simply by chewing more. It helped me reduce my belly flab to make myself feel happier and healthier. Crucially, though, it made sure I could appreciate my food more, chewing every last bite!

Eat Whole Grains

The first thing that I started to do when I became aware of how bad my health was eat more whole grains. Not only does eating more whole grain give your body better weight management and thus making it easier to get rid of that gut, but it helps to reduce other problems with your health too. For example, you can reduce inflammatory illnesses, you can lower blood pressure, you can handle your teeth better and you even reduce the risk of colorectal cancer.

By using whole grains like cereals in your life, you can find it much easier to live on a balanced and happy diet. It also helps to reduce things like diabetes, heart disease and strokes. This is going to ensure that you can live a happier and healthier life which is healthier in general. Lots of people find that by eating whole grains – and I found this, too – that their overall stamina improves.

They give you a great source of energy and nutrients, making them useful for those who want to get into shape ASAP. I used whole grains a lot in my food as soon as I discovered what they offer, and it has since then made it easier and more effective than ever to look after my body.

I found it easier to eat enticing meals that were good for me and gave me lots of benefits. It also meant that my belly size was being naturally reduced as I ate less damaging products.

Add Seeds to Your Salad

Given that the plan is to get our bellies nice and flat, it might not shock you to know that you should be eating more salads. Whilst we usually only use seeds to top off muffins, we should be eating far more seed than we do at present. Seeds are an excellent way to add wonderful flavour to a salad as well as create more texture, better quality and far more nutrition.

Adding seeds to your salad makes a big difference as it ensures you can get a better health kick. Throwing in some Chia seeds or Hemp seeds will give your body a lot of help in learning how to manage this part of the process.

Seeds, though, are perfect for upping nutrition and making it easier to get more bang for every piece of food that you might eat.

Seeds are great for those who are allergic to nuts as well. It means you can get lots of goodness with are healthy for us. They add a good way of having quality food in your diet as they are just loaded with good fats, vitamins and minerals. This will make it easier to look after your body long-term.

By simply sprinkling a few seeds into your baked goods or even just salads as suggested, you'll be doing your body a huge favour. It's yet another good way to start eating healthier and removing your need to go and get disgusting snacks like cheeseburgers and gut building chocolate snacks.

Introduce Avocado to your Diet

In my early weeks and months of changing my lifestyle and eating better to remove my belly, I tried a lot of different foods. One food that I came across that was going to be very good for me was Avocado.

This tantalizingly tasty and charming food is just what you need if you want to have a flat belly. Besides, in our later meal plan we will be suggesting you eat this quite a bit so make sure you start picking it up if you want to follow this plan and make it most likely to see progressive change.

However, the main reason to eat Avocado and use it as a way to empower your body is the fact that this is a major source of MUFA. This means that you also create more beta-sitonesterol, which is the anti-cholesterol. Now you can begin to work back against the damage that all of those pizzas and pies has caused!

Avocado is a great tasting product that you can use to make sure you have a wonderfully diverse diet, as well. They make a great selection to have as part of your diet and ensures you can see progressive change starting today.

Not only is this a wonderfully tasty product but it's very easy to get. You can find Avocado cheaply in stores and then can use it to make interesting dishes and to have as a snack. However you intend to eat it, though, you should definitely be introducing Avocado!

Stop Drinking Soda

Most of us who are used to living a "normal" life – me included – like soda. I used to have a real hankering for Sprite. However, with the amount of sugars in a can of soda I had to cut it out.

It was probably my biggest sin and all those empty, dead carbs just contribute to your body running on nothing. No wonder my gut started to get so big – I fed it on a diet of McDonalds with Sprite!

Naturally, this becomes a major health issue. To make sure you can begin to make proper changes to your lifestyle and quality of life in general, it might be a good time to leave that soda habit behind once and for all. Many people ruin their body and their teeth by drinking the stuff in place of water.

Start drinking mineral water instead and I guarantee you'll see a tremendous difference. Your body will look and feel fresher, you will start to feel refreshed more, and you won't be as dehydrated. Given that soda is usually just dehydration in a bottle, you won't help your body one bit by drinking soda.

You're making yourself more dehydrated and will be giving your body all the help it needs to keep ballooning up. This is a simple one to fix, really. For a flat belly, you need to cut out the soda. I get that it tastes wonderful, but it is the very opposite of what you should be hydrating yourself with.

Keep Non-Vegetable Carbohydrates Down

One of the most useful ways you can help your body, though, comes from how you eat and what you are taking in. With non-vegetable carbs you are merely just adding to the chance of your body ballooning up. Whilst most people are happy to keep eating pasta and bread, you will find that these non-veg carbs are going to just cause you problems as you try and get yourself into your ideal shape.

Try and stick to vegetables that are non-starchy and have just around 5g of carbs per serving. This is going to mean you can east healthier and keep the belly down. The likes of corn, potatoes, green peas and beets are very starchy forms of veg and thus will likely not be the best solution for you. I used to eat lots of potato, but have since cut down on the amount I eat by a significant margin.

I thought it was important to make this change as, without it, I'd probably still be making the same blind mistakes. Instead, try and turn to things like Romaine lettuce, bell peppers and asparagus. These all provide you with a simple and effective solution that is likely to keep your body nice and healthy.

By using this you also get a much more likely source of beneficial vitamins into your system. If a flat belly is what you wanted, like I did, then making sure you eat the right veg is just as important as eating veg in any form!

Eat Fiber

The best thing that you can do for your body when you want to get into shape and lose a flat belly is to eat more fiber. Fiber is very good for us and it is one of the few foods that our bodies can take in that will make us feel full as it's digested differently from other foods.

Eating fiber is so important for us – it gives our body some very important nutrients and makes life in general much easier for us. For those who want to get a flat belly, using fiber helps to reduce your need to eat.

You can get fiber in many sources – I found that cereals like Weetabix was a good solution for fiber introduction to my system. However, I also found that water-based fiber supplements like Fybogel was an excellent solution for the same problem.

Whatever you feel you need, you can find that taking in my fiber will help you get to where you want to be. Eating fiber is important for giving our body a very important nutrient, but it becomes even more important when you factor in that it stops us from eating, thus avoiding belly growth.

Consume Probiotic Supplements

The last part of your overall eating plan should be to start using probiotic supplements on a regular basis. These can be bought online, from health stores, and even found in some yogurts. Probiotics are good for the body as they help us create the kind of good bacteria that our bodies need. The more positive bacteria you get from a probiotic supplement, the healthier your gut is going to be.

Many people put their guts under immense strain for no real reason, and this can really harm your overall quality of life. A damaged gut is one that leads to many illnesses – most of our problems start in the gut, after all.

Therefore if you want to live a healthier and happier life, and you want to have a flat belly, probiotics will help. They won't help you lose weight, per se, but they make the perfect environment possible for your supplements to really work in your favour.

One thing you will find with probiotic supplements, though, is the variety. I used to buy many different brands to try them out but I typically found that Bimuno Powder was one of the best supplements on the market that was affordable and done what it claimed.

Probiotics is another extra that you can put to good use during a time when you want to try and get your health to the most optimum levels that you can. All that you need to do is pick them up and take them regularly for a healthier gut in the future.

Alright, now we know what to expect when it comes to our overall eating plans, habits and ideas. Now, we should take a look at why exercise plays such a critical role in seeing success in your aims for a flat belly, as exercises will be crucial to your success.

Exercises with Stability Ball

OK, so let's first take a look at the power of the exercise ball.

I found quite quickly into my fitness plans that using an exercise and stability ball was so important. I break down later on some of the main exercises to consider using with an exercise ball, but there are many to think about and consider. I found a list of excellent exercises with stability balls to try out on Greatist.

Check it out and use some of the ideas in there to help you start making positive and progressive change to the quality of your life long-term.

I found that by using a stability ball when exercising that my overall capacity for improvement grew. Instead of having to find compromises and weird solutions for trying to get fit, I would use these exercises. The ball made sure I was never having to compromise on performance, ensuring that I could just use the ball to do exercises as I intended.

The best one for me was the Wall Squat, personally. I found that using this was so powerful and helped me work on my quads, one of my weakest assets. If you want a flat belly then the rest of your body has to be ready to take on the brunt of the force whilst you work and try to get yourself into the best shape possible.

Therefore, using a stability ball you can work on everything else alongside that belly for a more balanced, comfortable fitness regime.

Alternating Fitness

Later on in this book I'll let you know about the kind of fitness training that I was undertaking to get into shape. I was using both cardio training and strength training, but I have to tell you guys the truth...

For six weeks, I was wasting my time entirely. Instead of trying to balance out my fitness and give my body both a rest on working on certain parts of the body, I foolishly tried three weeks strength/three weeks fitness. The end result was a body that was in total hormonal flux – I felt TERRIBLE!

Instead of seeing the gains I was hoping for, I noticed my body felt like it had been shot. I was noticing major problems with my body being out of sync as my fitness was out of touch with my strength. I then noticed that my strength work was decreasing when doing my cardio as my body was so used to the fitness workouts involving strength.

Basically, in essence, I nearly wasted all that time and put my body out of sync as well. This naturally made it much harder for me to train as I had wanted and it greatly reduced my overall potential for better involvement later on down the line.

As soon as I started to listen to the experts and began alternating from day-to-day, I found it far more effective. I break down my 14-day fitness plan that helped me later on, and you'll notice that in that no two days lead into the same kind of regime – balance is better, simple.

Planks, Not Crunches

A valuable companion for anyone looking for a flat body should be not be Crunches, but Planks. I found that these wonderfully astute exercises worked miracles for me in helping my body become more solid. It helps to strengthen the core and the legs, meaning that your flat belly won't be left looking out of shape with the rest of your overall shape.

Planks are easy to manage – and you can see how to take them on with the web in a matter of seconds. Crunches are equally easy but the reason we suggest potentially leaving them out is that they can be really bad for your back.

As you can see from the link above, it's a bad idea to rely on Crunches if you have back issues already. As a tall person in general I found that crunches benefited me on the day but I tended to pay for that pain later on down the line.

If you have a strong enough core to do planks then you should turn to them. Even then, planking in the early stages will toughen up that core and help you to plank more effectively. It will take you some time to get used to planking, but it is much safer for the body than crunching I found.

Plank is becoming better for keeping the body straight and building more general balance – it does not subject muscles to an overly strenuous set of muscle strains and makes your overall comfort far more likely.

Arm Exercises for Flat Belly

One major issue that I found when working out and preparing my body was the major issue of having strong, effective arm exercises to fall back on. Having good exercises that you can trust to give your body more solidity is important. I noticed quite quickly how big the gap between my much flatter belly and my flat arms were – I looked hideous.

So, I decided to take part in using Pullover exercises. Pullovers, when used for the arms, can be very powerful in helping to avoid your arms from getting too thin to go with the new belly. This is also good as Pullover exercise work other parts of the body, too, meaning that it's easier to get that flat belly.

Basically, you need to start off by getting a medicine ball, and done on a balancing ball. Lie on top of your balance ball with your knees bent, and shoulders centred on the ball. Keep your feet flat on the floor. From there, you need to hold the medicine ball against your chest, contract your abs as you push the medicine ball into the air above yourself. Lower your arms behind the head, before returning to your starting position.

I would do this for 15 reps at a time and over the course of a week or so, the difference was insane. It really helped me build up endurance in my arms but also helped me get to grips with using arm exercises.

Leg Exercises Flat Belly

I was always worried about working on my belly, and the end result being a flat belly and a flat body elsewhere that looked out of sync. So, I decided to try using an exercise recommended by a friend who had legs like brick walls – the Kettlebell Swing.

This basically means that you take the kettlebell and swing it between the legs. It will work your glutes, hips and quads so therefore making your legs much stronger as time goes on. What it takes to do this, though, is a hell of a lot of energy and power.

You'll find that both core and legs get great work to pull this off but it will be very hard to do at first without feeling the burn entirely. I found the best way to do this was to bend the hips, and hold the kettlebell with both hands at arm's length in front of me. Then, rock back a bit and use a hiking motion to put it between the legs.

Now, squeeze those glutes and thrust the hips forward forcefully and swing the weight back up to shoulder height. Reverse the motion and keep doing it until you feel like you have it spot on. It's obviously much easier to see than read about, so make sure you check out some Kettlebell Swing videos online.

It's a hard trick to describe but the actual form and what it entails is very easy to do once you see it in action – check it out, and benefit!

Back Exercises for Flat Belly

As I began to find success in my endurance training and my overall planning, one problem kept coming back to me – I was making the same mistakes over and over again. I kept only working on my abs and my belly, not the rest of my core. In turn I noticed a really big difference between my back and my abs.

So, I decided to start using a fitness exercise known as "Archer Row". Archer Row is great for improving posture and to ensure that your gut is going to be flatter much quicker. By using Archer Row, you improve your core power and the muscles in your back all at once. Given that I work with computers quite a lot, I spend a lot of time sitting in a recliner chair. So, you can imagine how much I needed to use this – my posture was shot!

All you need to do for a successful Archer Row is grab a dumbbell. Then, get into the push-up position with your hands under the shoulders and your body in a straight line from head to heel. Then. Separate the feet so they are wider than hip with, and turn them so that both point to your left.

From there, with your right palm on the floor, hold the dumbbell up high on your land hand to perform the row. Don't rotate with the dumbbell, though, or it will kill all the benefits of this exercise regime.

Abs Plank Exercises

A really powerful form of fitness exercise and training that I came across – and 100% loved – was to be using planking. Planking was huge a few years ago and whilst I used to laugh at people doing it, now I see why. Planking gives our body's greater strength and endurance, and also ensures that we are working on toning up those abs something awful.

Planking isn't easy by the way – it takes a LOT of work to get it right. This means usually taking hours' worth of training just to balance yourself. I spent more than my fair share of time just falling over and hurting myself!

Get that out of the system, though, and abs planking is so effect. The incredible strain it takes to keep yourself balanced using just your abs is very tough. The sheer intensity of trying to hold your own body weight suspended in the air with just this is going to be put a bit of a strain on your body.

However, what it done for me was improve both my confidence in my body, and my endurance. I was now able to take more stress and strain on the abs as they got used to holding so much weight. This made it much easier when getting into other forms of fitness training.

The endurance that you receive from getting good at managing your abs is something that you should definitely use to your advantage – a few planking sessions per day will do you the world of good.

Add Boxing to Your Routine

As I began to build up and lose that belly, one thing I noticed quite quickly was that I lacked a form of fitness I found fun. It all just felt like work – in my mind (and your own most likely) seeing exercise as work kills motivation. If you are just home from a 12-hour shift, or you have that one day off per week you get, you don't want to be "wasting" it by getting fit!

Whilst this is a terrible mentality to take if you want a flat belly, I know how easy it can be to lack that motivation. Therefore, adding boxing in can be good for the days when you need a more enjoyable way to tone up.

Boxing is great for building a flat belly as you become stronger, faster and fitter all at once. It works your arms and your excellently and improves the command you have over your arms and legs. This means that when it comes to strength training that will really help you shift that belly, your time spent boxing will get you used to the strain and the impact.

Boxing naturally toughens up arms and legs, too. This means you'll find it easier to cope with the endurance needed to get fit. For me, though, boxing was all about adding a bit of major excitement to my routine. It made those days where I had very little left in me a bit more fun, using boxing as stress management and fitness training!

Posture Improvement

A significant factor that I found when working out was that my posture had to improve. I actually thought that my posture was OK, but a friend who works as a fitness instructor helped me out one day. He noticed that, when doing strength training, I was "cheating" by arching my back and having poor posture.

Not only did this reduce the work needed by changing my back from being total straight, lessening the effect of my work, but it increased my chances of hurting myself. Having a total straight back during strength training is utterly vital. I know that extra tire might be pulling you forward a bit, but you have to work at improving this.

For one, having the right kind of posture makes it much easier to hit your targets. When you are working from the correct kind of stance you will notice just how easier it is to get a high, consistent tempo of work going.

This is really important but it's something that lots of people working out will underestimate. If you want to get the most out of your fitness and your body in general, then you absolutely need to improve your posture. At first, I had a friend "set" me and hold my back straight until I got used to doing it naturally.

If you are a natural sloucher then you will need help changing your nature way of leaning. It takes time, but if you're serious about getting a flat belly, that straight back becomes more important.

Pre-Workout Caffeine

A very useful tip that I found when working out was that having an extra cup of coffee before I started was a helpful little system. Many people don't do this as they fear suffering a crash when they are working out, but I found that it usually helped me get through the toughest parts of the workout.

It might just be my mentality, but I always found it hard to get started. Once I did get going, however, I tended to find that I would fly through the workout. That extra cup of coffee would give me the sprightly energy needed to get through that first crucial part. If you are like me and you have good staying power but struggle to actually get going in the first place, then this is a good tip for you to use.

Also, using caffeine is good as it can be an appetite suppressant. This helps you rip through without noticing the effects of hunger quite so badly. Whilst you will obviously still need energy to give you the power to complete the workout, most people find that having that little boost of energy can be enough to propel them through.

It's vital that you start your workout properly, as the level of energy you commit at the beginning will set the tone for the rest of that session. Therefore, using a coffee to boost you up and help you hit those targets quite quickly is very useful. It will help you avoid reckless investment of energy or not putting in the right effort from the beginning.

14 Day Flat Belly Eating Schedule

Of course, like anyone else who wants to get a flat belly, your most likely next requirement is going to be working on a flat belly eating schedule. I have provided you with a list below of an eating schedule that you should check out. However, it is just a guide. In this guide I've left you names of the kinds of foods I was eating, but one issue does exist here.

As someone with a genuine love for cooking and someone who has been involved for many years, I have very specific recipes. I also have a very particular way of cooking. Therefore, I would recommend that you look around for various ways to eat each of the meals I'll suggest. The best part about flat belly eating is that so long as we stick to the dishes, we should be fine.

That being said, I've also included another great diet plan that I found for you to look at. This Good to Know UK plan by the wonderful Sarah Allard should help. This will assist in helping you see just what you can do if you want to go down an alternative route. Every dish that I advise trying below, though, can easily be found online.

Again, it all comes down to personal taste. I love all of the dishes suggested below, but not everyone will. Even if you do like them, you might not like the specific way that I would have created the dishes. For this reason, I really do recommend you experiment moving forward. Experimentation allows you to get dishes that taste spectacular but really do fit with the kind of cooking style you love.

So, get creative! If you don't want to get creative, though, try the plan below. It worked for me and if you want to use it, you'll really benefit.

Day	Meal Type	Meal
1	Breakfast	Veg Frittata
1	Lunch	Whole Grain Burritos
1	Dinner	Southwest Spaghetti Squash
2	Breakfast	Toast and Egg and Avocado
2	Lunch	Peanut Butter on Tortilla
2	Dinner	Turkey Burgers
3	Breakfast	Oats
3	Lunch	Lettuce Wraps
3	Breakfast	Salmon /w Asparagus
4	Breakfast	Breakfast Bowl /w Sweet Potato, Chicken and Greens
4	Lunch	Tuna Avocado
4	Dinner	Greek Salad
5	Breakfast	Banana, Blueberry and Greens Smoothie
5	Lunch	Bento Box or Fruit Dippers
5	Dinner	Steak Kabob
6	Breakfast	Parfait with berries and oats
6	Lunch	Greek Salad on Pita
6	Dinner	Cauliflower Stir Fry
7	Breakfast	Pumpkin Oatmeal
7	Lunch	Quesadilla /w coconut oil
7	Dinner	Quinoa Bake
8	Breakfast	Banana Pancakes using Flax Seed
8	Lunch	Fruit Pizza
8	Dinner	Tacos /w lettuce wraps
9	Breakfast	Egg Cups
9	Lunch	Hummus with Raw Veg
9	Dinner	Stuffed Bell Peppers
10	Breakfast	Coconut Flakes, Chopped Fruit and Milk /w nut butter.
10	Lunch	Cucumber Stackers
10	Dinner	Crusted Quiche

11	Breakfast	Leftover Quiche
11	Lunch	Chicken Salad
11	Dinner	Soup /w Whole Grain Bread
12	Breakfast	Berry Smoothie
12	Lunch	Rice Cakes and Honey
12	Dinner	Fish with Parchment
13	Breakfast	Almond Flour Muffin
13	Lunch	Deli Pizza
13	Dinner	Shrimp /w Zoodles
14	Breakfast	Savoury Breakfast Bowl /w chia seeds and hemp hearts.
14	Lunch	Sweet Potato
14	Dinner	Fish in Parchment

As you can probably see, the above plan should be relatively simple to follow, and easy enough to enjoy. When you use this you are far more likely to get something that fits with your own dietary philosophy. Again, experiment with recipes that you know and that you can find online; the foods I have suggested are all quite expansive!

14 Day Flat Belly Exercise Schedule

For anyone looking to get into shape, then, you have a few options open to you. I personally found that using this routine of exercise for a 14-day period helped me to really start working on my abs and getting that belly fat down. My major problem was finding the time to exercise, though, and for most people this is likely to be the same problem.

If you want to avoid these problems then you can try out this 14-day workout plan to see what it does for you. I found that, throughout the lifespan of the workout routine, that I was really capable of making a major difference to the quality of life facing me. Within just a few short days I felt more alive and energized, and it helped me also find my baseline level of fitness.

If you are someone who worries about their health and weight, then this 14-day exercise regime should help you sort those problems out.

IMPORTANT – *Before we break down the fitness table below, make sure you read this next section. To make reading of the table easier, we've broken down an easy way for you to understand and appreciate what each fitness title will mean.*

Since we are using basic headlines here, you need to refer to what is below. I used each of these plans myself and found they had a huge amount of positive effect on me.

Cardio Workout

The kind of cardio exercises that we want you to be engaging with are very easy. It can be anything from using a cardio machine at the gym to cycling, walking or jogging. We won't be specific as all work out for you well. At the beginning and end of all cardio workouts, do a 5 minute set of stepping from side to side. The Cardio Workout involves;

- The first routine is a 3-minute warm-up, then a moderate to brisk paced workout that lasts 40-55 minutes. Then, you cool down at the end for 2 minutes with an easy paced version.

- The second routine involved a 3-minute warm-up, then a brisk 3-minute warm-up then a very few 2-minute routine. Alternate between brisk and fast 5-7 times, then cool down for 2 minutes. This should last around 35-45 minutes.

Belly Workout

Working that belly is going to take a fair bit more work and precision, though. You need cardio to cope with what is to come here, but the exercises themselves are fairly simple. In the belly workout plan you will 12-15 reps of each of the exercises we will list.

To do these, you should warm up for 3-5 minutes by simply going from side to side on your feet to warm up. You'll also need an 18-22" stability ball. It all depends on your height, so ask at the sporting store what ball will be best for you.

The exercises that worked for me most effectively are the following;

- **Reverse Crunches**
- **Rock & Roll**
- **Curls /w Ball**
- **Piking**
- **Skying**

Each of the above videos can be managed by simply going to YouTube. You'll find a video showing you there how to perfectly execute each of these. I would recommend videos to watch, but everyone learns best from their own sources. These are common stability exercises, though.

Day	Exercise Regime
1	Cardio Routine #1
2	Belly Workout Plan
3	Cardio Routine #2
4	Belly Workout Plan
5	Cardio Routine #1
6	Belly Workout Plan
7	Cardio Routine #2
8	Belly Workout (Twice)
9	Cardio Routine #1
10	Belly Workout (Twice)
11	Cardio Routine #2
12	Belly Workout (Twice)
13	Cardio Routine #1
14	Belly Workout (Twice)

If you want to make sure that your future is going to be a fit and healthy one, then this basic routine above should be enough to get you started. Not only should this make it a whole lot easier to go from A to B in terms of your fitness, but it will help you maintain those flat abs we were talking about.

By using this and the eating plan, alongside the rest of the tips in this book, I literally transformed my life. I've never felt healthier and happier, and you can be the same starting from today!

Thank you

I hope you enjoyed the book. I will appreciate your honest review on this book. Your feedback is important.

Join us on www.Personalitydevelopmentamstery.com

30842408R00026

Printed in Great Britain
by Amazon